CARNIVOROUS PLANTS

Sylvia A. Johnson, Series Editor

Translation of original text by Chaim Uri

The publisher wishes to thank Robert E. Lyons,
Assistant Professor of Horticulture,
Virginia Polytechnic Institute and State University,
for his assistance in the preparation of this book.

LIBRARY OF CONGRESS CATALOGING IN PUBLICATION DATA

Overbeck, Cynthia.
  Carnivorous plants.

    (A Lerner natural science book)
    Adaptation of: Shokuchū shokubutsu/by Kiyoshi
Shimizu.
    Includes index.
    Summary: Describes the Venus flytrap, sundew, pit-
cher plant, and bladderwort, and explains how active
and passive traps work in these meat-eating plants.
    1. Insectivorous plants—Juvenile literature. [1. In-
sectivorous plants. 2. Plants] I. Shimizu, Kiyoshi, 1924-
ill. II. Shimizu, Kiyoshi, 1924- Shokuchū shokubutsu.
III. Title. IV. Series.
QK917.O9413   583′.121   81-17234
ISBN 0-8225-1470-2 (lib. bdg.)   AACR2

International Standard Book Number: 0-8225-1470-2
Library of Congress Catalog Card Number: 81-17234

1 2 3 4 5 6 7 8 9 10 90 89 88 87 86 85 84 83 82

CARNIVOROUS PLANTS

by Cynthia Overbeck

Photographs by Kiyoshi Shimizu

A Lerner Natural Science Book

Lerner Publications Company ▪ Minneapolis

A black fly hovers in the air over a strange-looking plant. Attracted by a sweet smell, the fly lands on the flat, reddish surface of one of the plant's leaves. It begins to crawl across. Suddenly, the leaf moves! Before the fly can get away, the two halves of the leaf close around it. Two rows of "teeth" clamp together. All escape is cut off. The fly struggles to free itself, but the trap only closes more tightly. Soon, the fly is dead. In a few days, there is nothing left but the hard parts of its body.

This unlucky insect has become food for one of the world's most exotic plants—the Venus flytrap. The flytrap is one of about 450 species, or kinds, of carnivorous plants. **Carnivorous** (kar-NIH-vor-us) means "meat-eating." A plant that is carnivorous actually traps and eats insects, spiders, and, in some cases, tiny animals like frogs and mice. Carnivorous plants have developed this special way of feeding themselves in order to live and grow in a particular kind of environment.

In order to survive, most plants must take in water and minerals from the soil. These elements are combined with carbon dioxide and energy from sunlight to make the food that plants need to grow. Nitrogen is one of the most important minerals needed for plant growth. For this reason, most plants grow best in places where the soil is rich in nitrogen.

But carnivorous plants grow in wet, low-lying swamps and marshes. Here the damp soil is nitrogen-poor. Plants that take in nitrogen through their roots cannot live in such soil. Carnivorous plants stay alive by getting nitrogen and other minerals from another source. These plants get minerals from the bodies of the creatures that they trap and kill. The special leaves of carnivorous plants allow them to catch and use this handy source of food.

How do these unusual plants work? First, they must lure, or attract, animals. Unlike a frog or a bird, a carnivorous plant cannot reach out and grab an insect. It must wait until the insect comes to it. For this reason, carnivorous plants have special ways of attracting insects and other animals.

A waterwheel plant

Some carnivorous plants give off a sweet smell like that of nectar, which attracts insects such as flies, bees, and ants. Others give off a smell of decay, to which flies and some other insects are equally attracted. Many carnivorous plants have bright colors and patterns that serve as lures. And a whole group has leaves covered with sparkling droplets that attract insects with bright color and light, as well as with a sweet smell.

Once an animal has been lured to the plant, it must be trapped. Generally, carnivorous plants have two main kinds of traps: **active,** or moving, traps and **passive,** or still, traps. Plants with active traps, like those of the Venus flytrap and the waterwheel (pictured above), have parts that move quickly to trap any insect that lands on them. The moving parts may clamp together like jaws. Or they may swing shut like a trapdoor.

Left: A sundew plant
Above: One type of pitcher plant

Passive traps do not depend on movement of their parts to trap animals. Some passive traps, like those of the sundews (above left), are sticky traps. Although some of them may move after they have caught an insect, the actual trapping is done by a sticky substance on their leaves. This substance catches and holds insects without the need for movement.

Other passive traps are the "pitfall" type. They are found in the pitcher plants like the one shown in the picture on the right. Inside the leaves of these plants are cleverly made one-way tunnels into which insects are lured by sweet nectar. Once they are inside, the insects cannot get back out.

All of these traps help to feed the plants on which they grow. Usually, many traps grow on one plant. They all work together to catch, digest, and absorb the nutrition that the plant needs to survive.

Left: The Venus flytrap
Above: The flowers of
the Venus flytrap

Perhaps the most familiar of the carnivorous plants is the Venus flytrap. This plant is found only in the United States, in the swamps of North Carolina. The entire plant grows about a foot (30 centimeters) tall. In spring it has pretty white flowers blooming on top of tall stalks. But the most interesting parts of this plant are its leaves.

The flytrap's narrow green leaves grow in a circle around the plant's base. Each leaf blade opens into two halves, almost like a clamshell. The two halves, or **lobes**, are attached to a center rib. Each lobe averages about an inch (2.5 centimeters) in length. The inside surfaces of the lobes are usually a reddish color. Around the curved outer edge of each lobe is a row of stiff, pointed bristles, called **cilia** (SIL-ee-uh). On the inside surface of each lobe are three "trigger" hairs.

This closeup picture of an open Venus flytrap leaf shows the tiny trigger hairs on its lobes.

The pictures on these two pages show the leaf of a Venus flytrap capturing a spider.

These strange leaves are the plant's traps. When the lobes are in an open position, the traps are set, ready for a meal. In the pictures above, a spider has been attracted by a leaf's red color and by the sweet smell of a nectar-like substance produced on its edges. As the spider crawls onto the leaf's surface, it disturbs the trigger hairs. This is the signal for the lobes to move. But the trap must receive two signals in order to close. It will react only if one hair is touched twice or if two hairs are touched. This is the plant's way of making sure that it has caught a live, moving creature and not a piece of grass or a leaf.

Once the double signal has been given, the lobes close quickly around the spider. The cilia lock together to prevent escape. At this point, a very small spider or insect could still crawl out from between the cilia. The plant rejects such tiny animals because it would use more of its energy to digest them that it would gain from their bodies in food value.

As the trap closes, a fluid begins to ooze out of the inner surfaces of the lobes, and the spider is drowned. The fluid contains **digestive enzymes** (EN-zimes), substances that change the spider's body material into a form that the plant can absorb as nourishment. As more and more enzymes flow into the trap, the spider's soft body parts gradually dissolve.

Another Venus flytrap catches an insect.

This Venus flytrap leaf has been opened to show the partly digested body of the spider it has trapped.

In 8 to 10 days, the body parts of the animal have become a nitrogen-rich liquid that is absorbed into the plant. The trap opens, and out fall the hard body parts that the plant could not digest. The trap is now set again. One trap will usually catch and digest an average of three meals before it withers and dies.

Opposite: The water-wheel plant floats under the surface of a pond.

Left: The swamp environment of the waterwheel plant. *Right*: The flower of the waterwheel.

Another carnivorous plant that uses an active trap much like that of the Venus flytrap is known as the waterwheel plant. It is found in Europe, Australia, India, Japan, and Africa. This small, rootless plant floats just under the surface of quiet ponds and swamps. The whole plant is only about 4 to 12 inches (10 to 30 centimeters) long. Its little white flowers, which bloom in the spring, show above the water's surface. The traps are underwater.

Each plant has a slender stem with leaves that are almost transparent. Groups of eight leaves are arranged around the stem like the spokes of a wheel. This is why the plant is called the waterwheel.

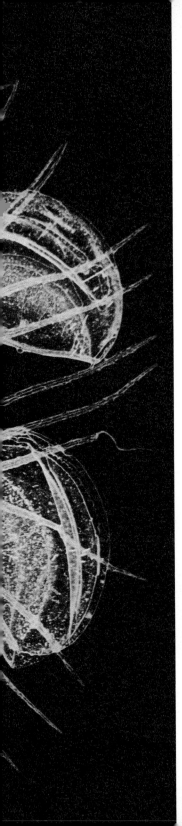

This picture shows a single leaf of the water-wheel plant greatly magnified.

Left: This special photograph shows a water-wheel plant from the end of its stem. You can see how the leaves are arranged in a wheel around the stem.

Left: A waterwheel plant with its leaves open. *Opposite*: This waterwheel leaf has caught an insect larva.

The waterwheel's leaves are its traps. Each leaf is very tiny—less than ¼ inch (6 millimeters) long. Such tiny traps can catch only very small creatures. The waterwheel feeds on water fleas, on **plankton**, or microscopic water animals, and on tiny **larvae** (LAR-vee)—insects in an early stage of development.

The waterwheel's leaves act just like underwater Venus flytraps. They have two lobes, rows of bristles, and trigger hairs inside their lobes. When an insect enters a trap, the halves snap shut in a fraction of a second. The waterwheel then digests its meal and reopens to catch the next one.

Both the Venus flytrap and the waterwheel plant use a clamping movement to trap animals. But another type of carnivorous plant with an active trap—the bladderwort—moves in a different way. The bladderwort has a kind of trapdoor for catching its meals.

Bladderworts are found in many parts of the world. Although some bladderworts grow on land, most grow in quiet ponds and swamps. Like the waterwheel plants, they do not have roots. They float in strands or clumps just below the water's surface. In summer, their tiny yellow or purple flowers bloom above the water.

Growing all along the bladderwort's thin stems are its leaves. Each leaf is actually a little air bag, or **bladder.** The bladders are very small; the biggest is only about $1/5$ inch (5 millimeters) long. These tiny, balloon-like leaves are the traps the bladderwort uses to catch water fleas, insect larvae, and sometimes small tadpoles.

At one end of each bladder are feathery hairs that serve as triggers. These hairs are arranged around an opening, across which is a tiny "trapdoor." This door swings open only one way—inward.

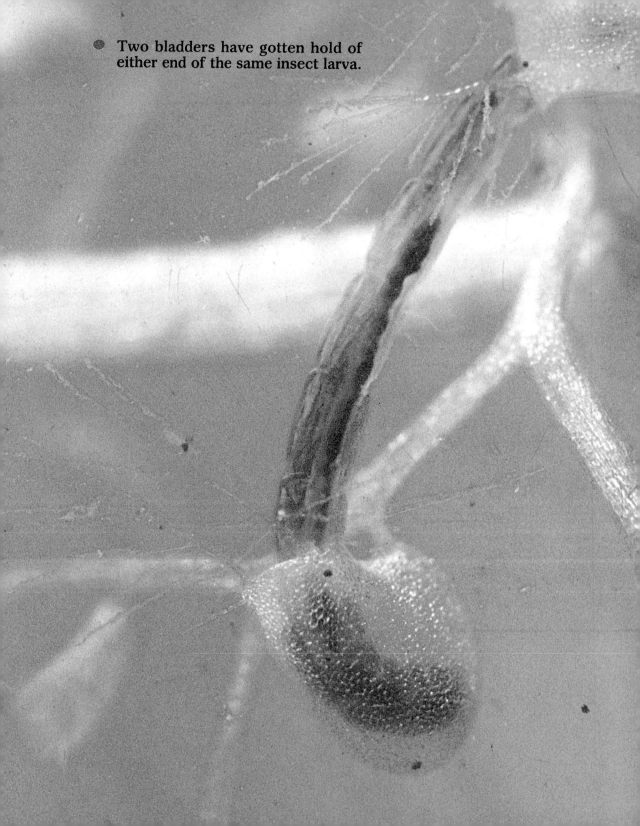

Two bladders have gotten hold of either end of the same insect larva.

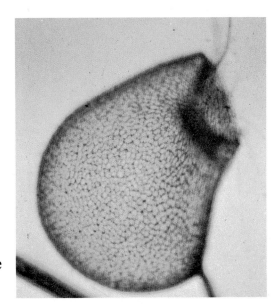

An enlarged picture
of a single bladder

To trap insects, the bladder uses suction. When the door is closed and the bladder is empty, its walls are limp and collapsed. Then an insect swims by and brushes against the trigger hairs. Suddenly the bladder walls expand. This forces the trapdoor open and creates a sucking action. As the walls expand, water rushes in, pulling the insect with it. Then the trapdoor slams shut, and the insect is caught inside the bladder.

Immediately the digestive enzymes inside the bladder go to work. If the insect is tiny, the bladder takes only 15 to 30 minutes to absorb the nitrogen and other minerals from its body. If the insect is larger, digestion may take up to 2 hours. Sometimes, a bladder gets hold of an insect or larva that is too large to fit inside it. Then it digests the meal bit by bit. A single bladder can catch and digest about 15 small creatures before it dies.

Left: **Sundews growing a-mong other marsh plants**
Above: **A sundew flower**

Flytraps, waterwheels, and bladderworts all use active traps to catch their food. But other carnivorous plants use passive traps—traps that do not depend on movement to capture insects. One group of plants, the sundews, uses a sticky trap.

The small roundleaf sundew provides a good example of the way a sticky trap works. This plant grows in many swampy areas of the world, including parts of the United States. The plant is small—about 3½ inches (8 centimeters) across. It is often partly hidden among taller weeds and plants that grow around it.

In summer the roundleaf's tall center stems carry white flowers. The leaves of the sundew look bright red. They seem to be covered with sparkling drops of dew. But what looks like a pretty red, dewdrop-covered leaf is really a deadly trap for flies and other insects.

A closeup view of the surface of a sundew leaf

The sundew's leaves are covered with many little stalks of different heights. At the top of each stalk is a tiny **gland,** or organ, that produces a clear, sticky liquid. This liquid forms a droplet on the tip of the stalk. Usually the gland is a reddish color, so the liquid on it appears to be red, too.

Flies and other insects are drawn to the sundew by the color and sparkling light, as well as by an attractive scent that the plant gives off. But when a fly lands on a sundew leaf, it is in trouble.

Immediately its feet are caught in the sticky liquid on top of the taller stalks. As the fly struggles to escape, more sticky liquid flows out of the glands. Now the fly is trapped for good. As in the pictures above, the stalks around the fly bend toward its body, giving off more liquid. The whole leaf curls slightly to cup the body. Digestive enzymes work until the soft parts of the fly have dissolved and become absorbed into the leaf. After four or five days, the leaf and stalks uncurl.

The pictures on these two pages show a fly being trapped and digested by a sundew leaf.

The spoonleaf sundew

The roundleaf sundew is only one of about 90 kinds of sundews found all over the world. Sundews may have leaves of different shapes—round, narrow, or threadlike. They may also vary quite a bit in size. Some African sundews are giants with leaves two feet (60 centimeters) long. They actually trap and digest small animals such as mice. But most sundews are much smaller.

One smaller type is the spoonleaf sundew. It is found in swampy areas throughout Asia, Australia, and the Philippines. Like all sundews, its leaves are arranged in a circle around a center, close to the ground. Growing up from the center is a tall stem. Flowers bloom atop this stem in the spring or summer.

The spoonleaf traps and digests animals in the same way that the roundleaf does. Since it is a very small plant with leaves about an inch (2.5 centimeters) long, it catches only tiny insects like gnats and lice.

All sundews have leaves with stalks tipped by liquid-producing glands like those of the roundleaf sundew. In all kinds, the actual trapping of the insect is done by the sticky liquid on the stalks. Once the insect is trapped, the stalks bend toward its body to surround it with digestive enzymes. In some sundews, the whole leaf curls around the insect during the digestion process.

Narrowleaf sundews growing among other swamp plants

A narrowleaf sundew in action

The narrowleaf sundew is one type that curls tightly around the animals it has caught. In the picture on the left, a spider has just been trapped by the sticky fluid of a narrowleaf sundew. The picture on the right shows the same leaf about eight hours later. It is now curled tightly around the spider as it digests the body.

Several varieties of this plant are found in both the United States and Japan. Usually its leaves are only about an inch (2.5 centimeters) long and less than ½ inch (1 centimeter)

A threadleaf sundew
leaf coiled around an
insect's body

wide. Yet they can often trap large insects like dragonflies
and butterflies by using teamwork. Several leaves on the same
plant actually work together, each one trapping a different
part of the insect's body.

Another kind of sundew that curls around trapped insects
is the threadleaf sundew. This is a tall, trailing plant with
long, very narrow leaves. Different varieties of threadleaf
sundews live in North America as well as in Asia, Africa,
and Australia. Even though the leaves look a bit different
from those of other sundews, they work in the same way.
They are covered with sticky-topped stalks that trap insects.
When a threadleaf sundew has caught a fly or gnat, its long
leaf may actually coil twice around the insect's body while
digestion is taking place.

These dragonflies were caught by their wings as they flew near the sticky leaves of a narrow-leaf sundew plant.

Another group of carnivorous plants that catches insects with sticky traps is the butterwort family. There are about 30 kinds of butterworts growing in North America and in some parts of Asia. Although most grow in swamps and marshes, the special type in these pictures grows high on rocky mountainsides in Japan. Like all butterworts, the fleshy green leaves of this plant grow close to the ground in a cluster. Growing out of the center are tall stems on which flowers bloom in spring or early summer.

The leaves of a butterwort plant

The leaves of the butterwort are its traps. They are small —about ½ inch (1.3 centimeters) long—so they can trap and digest only tiny insects like gnats or small ants. The surface of each leaf has two kinds of glands. One kind gives off an oily, sticky substance. This substance makes the leaves feel greasy, almost buttery, to the touch. It also has a musty smell that attracts insects.

Once an insect has crawled onto the leaf and gotten stuck, the edges of the leaf roll up to form a kind of cup. Then another set of glands begins to give off digestive liquid. The insect is killed, and its body is digested in a couple of days.

Some pitcher plants grow close to the ground *(left)*, while others grow on vines *(opposite)*.

Of all the carnivorous plants with passive traps, perhaps none are more exotic-looking than the pitcher plants. These plants have special leaves that are hollow and can hold water, almost like a real jug or pitcher. The leaves are the plant's traps. Their structure and appearance are so unusual that people have given them many fanciful nicknames, such as Devil's jug, huntsman's cup, and Indian dipper.

There are about 80 kinds of pitcher plants growing in the wetlands of the world. Many, like the North American pitcher plant shown above, grow close to the ground in a circle around a center base. All of the leaves of these plants are traps for catching insects.

Other pitcher plants are found in the tropical wetlands of Maylasia, Madagascar, and Sri Lanka. These plants have many brightly colored pitcher leaves growing on vines.

Three stages in the development of a pitcher leaf

These tropical pitcher plants have ordinary green leaves as well as brightly colored pitcher leaves. The pictures above show how their pitchers grow from a **tendril,** or threadlike stem. As the leaf grows, it swells to form a colorful "jug." The top opens to form a leafy hood. In some pitcher plants this hood is just a kind of frill around the pitcher's edges. In others it forms a flat "roof" above the whole opening.

The leaves of various kinds of pitcher plants may differ in size as well as in color, pattern, and shape. They can be from 2 inches (5 centimeters) to more than 2 feet (60 centimeters) tall. Small pitcher plants trap insects such as flies, beetles, and ants. The largest pitchers can also trap small frogs or mice. But whatever their size or outer appearance, all pitchers trap animals in basically the same way.

This x-ray picture shows a pitcher partly filled with water

A pitcher trap is passive; it does not need to move in order to trap an insect. Instead, its clever design becomes a prison for almost any insect that crawls into it.

The leaf forms a kind of tube. At the top is an opening, usually brightly colored. The bottom part of the tube is shaped like a cup. Rainwater collects in this cup. (In the pitchers that grow close to the ground, water is also drawn up from the soil to fill the cup.) In most types of plants, the hood above the opening helps to keep too much rainwater from coming in. This hood always stays open. It never snaps shut to trap an insect, as some people believe.

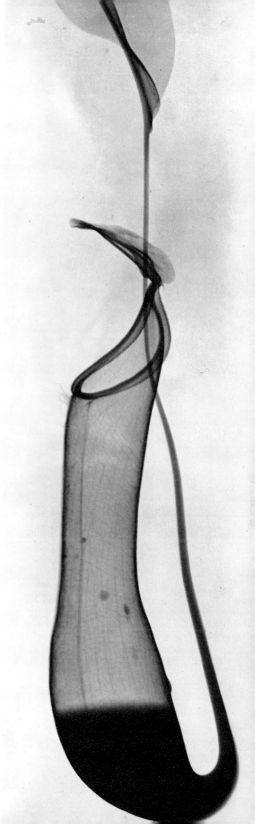

A sweet nectar is produced around the lip of the pitcher opening. Attracted by the nectar and the bright colors of the pitcher, an insect flies or crawls onto the convenient lip. It begins to sip the nectar and soon crawls further into the opening, searching for more.

When the insect moves into the tube of the pitcher plant, it is in trouble. The inside walls of the tube are slick and slippery as ice. The insect slips further down. There it finds its footing along hairs that line the lower part of the tube, as seen in the picture on the left. But the hairs all face downward, toward the pool of water below. Once the insect has crawled past them, it is impossible for it to get back up. The insect struggles but finally becomes exhausted and falls into the water below. There it drowns.

Now digestive enzymes flow into the pool. As in other carnivorous plants, the soft parts of the insect's body are digested and absorbed into the plant. The hard parts of the body collect in the bottom of the pitcher.

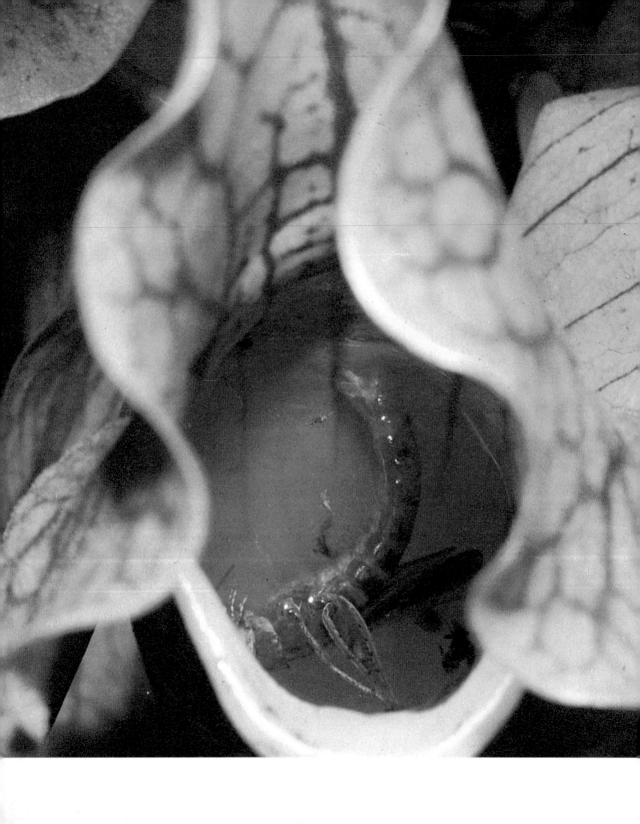

Opposite: This insect has drowned inside a pitcher plant. *Right*: This pitcher plant has been cut open so that you can see the remains of the insects that it has trapped and digested.

Pitcher plants, like all the carnivorous plants in this book, have found ways to thrive in places where most plants could not live. With the help of their strange and often beautiful leaves, they feed on the creatures that share their marsh environment.

But as hardy as carnivorous plants are, today the lives of many of them may be in danger. As people drain more and more marshland to make way for buildings and roads, the plants have fewer places to grow. They are becoming increasingly rare.

Today people are trying to grow some carnivorous plants in indoor greenhouses. In this way, they hope to preserve these fascinating and unusual plants and to make sure that they do not disappear from our world.

GLOSSARY

active trap—a trap that uses quick movement of its parts to catch insects or small animals that come in contact with its surface

bladder—an air sac that can be inflated or deflated

carnivorous—meat-eating

cilia—short, stiff bristles that grow on the edges of some carnivorous plant leaves

digestive enzymes—substances made by carnivorous plants that help to change the animals they trap into a form that can be absorbed

gland—a tiny organ that makes substances such as nectar and digestive juices in carnivorous plants

larvae—insects or animals in an immature stage of development, after hatching and before becoming adults. A tadpole is a *larva* of a frog.

lobes—the fleshy parts of some carnivorous plant leaves

passive trap—a trap that does not use movement of its parts to catch insects or small animals that come in contact with its surface

plankton—microscopic water animals or plants

tendril—a threadlike, coiling part of a plant

INDEX